FROM THE FIRE HILLS

Crab Orchard Series in Poetry
Editor's Selection

FROM THE FIRE HILLS

CHAD DAVIDSON

Crab Orchard Review &
Southern Illinois University Press
CARBONDALE

17 16 15 14   4 3 2 1

The Crab Orchard Series in Poetry is a joint publishing venture of Southern Illinois University Press and *Crab Orchard Review*. This series has been made possible by the generous support of the Office of the President of Southern Illinois University and the Office of the Vice Chancellor for Academic Affairs and Provost at Southern Illinois University Carbondale.

Editor of the Crab Orchard Series in Poetry: Jon Tribble

Library of Congress Cataloging-in-Publication Data
Davidson, Chad, 1970–
[Poems. Selections]
From the Fire Hills / Chad Davidson.
    pages cm. — (Crab Orchard Series in Poetry)
ISBN-13: 978-0-8093-3323-3 (paperback : alk. paper)
ISBN-10: 0-8093-3323-6 (paperback : alk. paper)
ISBN-13: 978-0-8093-3324-0 (ebook)
ISBN-10: 0-8093-3324-4 (ebook)
I. Title.
PS3604.A946A6 2014
811'.6—dc23   2013032648

Printed on recycled paper. ♻

The paper used in this publication meets the minimum requirements of American National Standard for Information Sciences—Permanence of Paper for Printed Library Materials, ANSI Z39.48-1992. ∞

for Gary Davidson

CONTENTS

IV

V

ACKNOWLEDGMENTS

Grateful acknowledgment is made to the editors of the following publications, in which poems from this book first appeared:

American Literary Review—"The Last Crusade"
Birmingham Poetry Review—"Limoncello," "San Luca," and "Waterwalkers"
Boston Review—"Survival Italian"
Copper Nickel—"Anthem"
Crab Orchard Review—"The Gothic Line," "In Ravenna," "Ossi di Morto," and "Truffle"
Green Mountains Review—"Bellagio," "Lovers in the Capuchin Crypt," "The Screaming Toddler in Santa Maria Novella," and "The Subjunctive Mood"
The Journal—"Hole in the Heart"
Michigan Quarterly Review—"Aerial"
North American Review—"The Churches of Italy" and "The Grief Industry"
Passages North—"The Grotesque"
A Poetry Congeries—"Blood Orange"
Ploughshares—"Labor Days"
River Styx—"Dispensation"
Sou'wester—"Pantelleria"
Subtropics—"Controlled Burn"
32 Poems Magazine—"Elegy," "Exile," "From the New Republic," and "Soft Costs"

Thanks to Gwen and Gary Davidson, Bob and Jane Hill, Eric Smith, Scott McDaniel, Jon Tribble, Allison Joseph, and everyone at Southern Illinois University Press. And to Gregory Fraser, John Poch, and Austin Hummell: if these poems seem at times as much yours as mine, that's because they are.

FROM THE FIRE HILLS

IN RAVENNA

Three boys, old enough to hurt someone,
young enough to think it doesn't matter,
sat outside the small green plot I came to.
Dante's grave. All of us pulled there,
experiencing gravity, out of control
for different reasons. I could not prepare,
really, for facing this, just as these boys—
smoking too deliberately, collars relieved
like rose petals from the extravagant
ceilings of basilicas—could not understand
their own indifference, or why they huddled,
stared when I walked by. They were a type
of beauty, as far as beauty is ignorant of itself,
disdainful of place: that casual square,
Franciscan façade, that entire city turning
under the swelter of an afternoon, June
in the marshlands to the east. Sometimes,
I stand in front of history and feel nothing.
Then, some wrecked mosaic, awkward
in the transom of a secondary church, behaves
just so, as if the artists thought of me and all
my imperfections. Sometimes, people gather
in the hearts of forgotten cities, and I hate them
for their nonchalance, the terror in their boredom.
They have been dying here for millennia, these boys,
and there is little I can do, on this casual trip
in the heat, map in hand, to guide them out.

I

THE GOTHIC LINE

That evening I must have crossed it, racketing out
the cobbles in an orange city bus to Casalecchio—
suburb of Bologna on the Reno's banks—
to dine with those I hardly knew, owners of the only
café near the school where every day I filled blanks
with proper nouns, conjugations in the remote past,
for which, I later learned, Italian now has little use.
What was I doing as I stamped my feet, then ticket,
ascended the stairs at the stop, huddled in my half
literacy and cheap coat I had to buy
when a winter I had not counted on descended?
I must have transgressed some checkpoint
between acquaintance and friend, grim shoreline
pocked with the unintelligible artifacts
of embarrassment and xenophilia, as Mina
buzzed me up to a linen table and the foreboding
of their furniture: *mobili* in Italian, the movables,
like me on the ride out of the urban, repeating
scant vocabulary to the cobble's stutter.

And it's not the tortellini served that night, handmade,
curled in silken broth, or the fizzy wine, which Dino—
from *Costante*, constant, forever—bottled himself.
Not even some idea of the exotic, which surely
I still felt then, one season into my becoming,
my beginning Italian like a wounded machine
sputtering its declensions to their transnational
sympathy, which, after all, could be anyone's.

But the grandfather, who arrived after dinner,
spoke a broken dialect gauzed in bookish Italian—
another kind of wound—whose eyes,
when Mina introduced me as *the American*,
glazed over then burned through me,
or the version of me forever fixed in his past,
in an Allied tank entering Bologna,
while he holed up in the hills near the Gothic Line,
his wife in labor, in a shelter outside the punished
city and the periodic sentences of bombing.

And though I confess now my ignorance
of war, that I first entered the vast cathedral
of its history in Bologna that winter, still
I knew enough to understand what he didn't say,
which, in my own tongue, sounds like this:
You, who liberated the streets in your machines,
who delivered my daughter from the fire hills
and noise of our wrongness, still I claim you,
blue-eyed bringer of the marketplace.
Hold my hand, as you are doing now,
as you will continue to do, your calling,
your curse—for you will occupy forever
one person to me, constant, immovable.

VANDALS

A babel of students crowds the café
facing San Francesco, late morning washed
in terracotta and European Top 40
from the boom box atop the pastry display.
Here, Mina and Dino manage cappuccino
for the Brits and Danes, the Japanese girl
with green hair and acne, a Parisian couple
smacking packs of Marlboros into palms,
all on break from language class, packed
too tight to open newspapers none of us
can read. Instead, we curse the hangover
in separate idioms, portion out our ignorance,
while the world turns around us, as Mina turns,
cramped behind the counter, lip-synching
the grotesque pop spasms of a Swedish band
in English in her own particular purgatory—
part lament for our monstrous Italian,
part redemption in our various attempts
at ordering, while we Vandals descended
each day, ran away the local businessman
nicknamed *la Pecora*—the Sheep—
and the Eritrean owner of a disco down the street,
who, though diminutive, smacked of royalty
untarnished by exile, which Mina must feel
as we flock again, open to the façade
of a church rebuilt from rubble, until she can't
take it any longer, *Basta, uffa, enough
with foreigners*, but instead cranks the radio

and spins like a record behind the counter.
And since I am caught in the eternal present
of my introductory Italian, I cannot understand
the remote past of her joy, so stand there,
cloistered in regret, unable to tell her *good day*
in any but the *Let's Go Italy* way.
But it is good, the sun throwing its conditional
all over the church, so I concentrate on the song,
its front man in full throes now of his imaginary
adolescence, calling for anyone to save him,
love him in any language admissible
by Nordic socialism. And I almost hear
the little motors of his bilingual clichés,
in all his talk of *rapture* and *ecstasy*,
which, in the mouth of a Swede, lip-synched
by Mina, in the amber morning
of my memory of that fall, hangs in the vaulted
interior of the café, at least in the church
I have made of it—some minor basilica,
destroyed in the fifth century, by Vandals.

SAN LUCA

As we climbed its porticos that fall,
the sun, gauzed and fretful, fell. Strange vigil
she kept with a lighter in her palm, dull
flame of lost faith. We were each other's Virgil,
I and a green-eyed Brazilian girl
who talked so much of God and all the rest
I swore it was the distance made her twirl
that cigarette between her fingers and guess
how many like us conquer the hill but never
enter. (The climactic anticlimax:
our arrival at that bolt and lever
fixed.) A nonbeliever and, thus, relaxed
with failure, still, in that failing day,
I could not help but think we lost our way.

LOVERS IN THE CAPUCHIN CRYPT

Just off the Via Veneto, a shady bend
all overpriced cafés and cops with Uzis,
remains of Capuchins, thousands of them,

line the chapels in a crypt, their hip bones
perfect wings for skulls; fingers, numbers
on the wondrous clock on the wall. Look closely

and it runs, *tempus fugit*, like this bald man
elbowing his way through gloom, a mouth-
breather bent on escape, who rushes past

the Russian couple in the one unossified nook.
No matter, for they are enjoying themselves
immensely, taking in the poorly rendered

prose, the baby bones of the Barberini,
marveling at the jaws that yawn parabolas
above their heads, as if time existed merely

for them, as if these monks, for centuries,
prepared for this, ensuring empty sockets
aimed at love. Absence, after all, is just

a well to fill. So the couple embrace—
there is no other word—and kiss and all,
smack dab in the middle of the horror.

And though the sassy woman working
postcards comes across the intercom
scolding the bald guy and his camera,

she says nothing to the lovers staring deep
into the ignorance of where they are headed,
in afternoon blur, wearing those outrageous colors.

THE SUBJUNCTIVE MOOD

When the Swedish girl, not even twenty,
played the part of Chiara asking if I needed more
pancetta for my Carbonara, I did not but said I did,
that the water was rolling now eight minutes, salty
and starched as the tide off Corpus Christi,
where a month ago I waded with someone
I had no intent to wait long for. What did I know
of *Carbonara*—some Roman affair
named for the coal miner's wife waiting
for a husband's return from the underworld,
the dish formed with cheese Boccaccio praised,
and yolks from the eggs of turmeric-fed hens,
pasta requiring the subjunctive mood: hopeful
like the wife summoning her man back
to bright street markets wearing the raiment
of capitalism and cancer and a hunger for her?

And yet I am there at the unearthing, the excavation
of that distant fall in language school, descending
again to advanced conversation and the Swede
hip to grammatical gender, those green-blue eyes
and ease with which she conjured cappuccino.
I rose from the intermediates—a military brat
from Canada who always tanked declensions,
the Japanese girl shuffling in her flip-flops—
to the Bundesrepublik of third level,
overrun with Germans, a Gothic Line
of dative case and remote past wizards.

How I envied their constant voiceovers,
hushed collaborations, conspiratorial, the rush
to resuscitate a fellow national gone cold
midsentence, while I waded through the murky
dialogues with no intermittent oil lamps
of linguistic aid, no native speaker tugging
the imaginary rope I wanted to be tied to and with,
whose name, were I to choose, would have been
Courtney—some fine American strain to follow
to the surface. Instead, I pined like a coal miner
for that Swedish girl and any comprehension
of the scenario, for then Chiara and I
priced oleanders for the garden, and Salvo
at the nursery was a giant prick pushing
the camellias instead. This, a situation
the Germans mastered, grabbing Salvo
by the scruff of his patently southern dialect
to conjugate a bargain out of him.

All the while, their subtle, simultaneous
translation transformed our textbooks
into some chic, far-flung district of Berlin
in summer, where every flower offered its bloom
in the proper tense, and the dogs all barked
in Swedish. And it is not because the Germans
saved themselves from shame dressed in silence,
though that is what I thought then,
but rather the opposite: that they could never
know the gasp, the suffocating precision
of my ignorance in that language class,
in Bologna, and the odd love I felt
for the Swede and the Chiara inside her,
wondering which of the two labored harder,
and for Salvo: a stereotype in my book,
hopeless lover of the slow *Mezzogiorno*,
who must hate the barbarians in the gutters

of their gutturals, their glottal stops
and fricatives. Salvo: some character
whose name even means he is saved,
means he wears as work only loam, spared
the mines from which his brothers or cousins,
bathed in a second kind of night, returned
to wives—call them all Camellia—whose pity
reeked of pork fat, who cracked the eggs,
grated cheese, and spoke only in the simple
present, daunted by the irony of the subjunctive,
a difficult mood, botched even by natives,
implying hope, yes, but also doubt,
fear, and the marigold's nauseating blush.

THE SCREAMING TODDLER IN
SANTA MARIA NOVELLA

In any of the many Madonna and Childs I have seen,
the infant Jesus, in byzantine luster or plain pastel,
is mute, dizzyingly superior, watching watchers
with a glint of all to come. But how could he know,
on this day in Florence, birthplace of most things
good, a child with mop hair would bang
the small hammers of her feet on a metal ramp
and praise the miracle of this, her own bipedalism,
in scream. The mother, a doubter, had moved on
to the gift shop, snatching up snapshots of a screamless,
daughterless church all spiritus and carved wood,
the Gothic columns candyish, lovely. The father, yea,
as is customary in Christendom, was absent, or busted
by the squat, overzealous guard for breach of photograph.

Yet they must have heard this tiny thing turn
our church into a Vandal sack, conquer cry,
and turned away, as Judas does in a Last Supper
I saw and was moved by—the quietude of betrayal,
the elegance. Then again, we sing and praise
and ring too many bells for a clock that learns
the hour, for the birthday of some martyr of anything,
because there is one for each of the nonmiraculous
days between, and one for this little headache
of a child too young to understand her own beatitude,
Susie, let us call her, whose namesake saint
of annoyance on Saturday was screamed at until
reunited, in the year of our Lord 1294, amen.

CONTROLLED BURN

The brown hills of California are on fire
again, the desert scrub, burning bush.
On television, the host of a cooking show
breaks down the cuisine of Pantelleria.
We had to set fire to the hills, wrote Mussolini's son
of Ethiopia. *The fields and little villages.*
That was 1936. Today, we celebrate
Pantescan food and its Moorish influence.
Influenza in Italian. In my California,
planes hauled nothing but water. Helicopters
buzzed the high villages. The stink of ash.
Swimming pools dusted in it. On Pantelleria,
capers are picked by hand. Every day begins
and ends with kneeling. I held my hand
to my forehead, surveying the hills with my father.
He steadied the hose to soak the roof.
I was seven, I was scared, I was his son.
After the racks were emptied, wrote Bruno Mussolini,
I began throwing bombs by hand. Now,
the host plays bocce with three old men
on a dirt field. This is the moving part, a touching
story, some human interest. *The bombs hardly touched
the earth before they burst into white smoke.*
The red ball knocks the green ball out of play.
A close-up of the contact seems inevitable.
Was it smoke or cloud that blotted out the sun
of my childhood, when I returned home wheezing
and my mother boiled water? Ten men sit around

an enormous pot. Capers fall from the blisters
of a picker's hands. The camera trains.
Now that's what I call living, the host says.
With a damp towel over my head, I swallowed steam.
The dry grass began to burn, wrote Mussolini's son.
I thought of the animals: God, how they ran.
The host is now on a Vespa. *Wasp* in Italian.
He is having a ball. *It was most amusing*,
wrote Bruno of the bombing of Ethiopia.
Surrounded by a circle of fire, five thousand
Abyssinians came to a sticky end. Abyssinia
and Ethiopia are roughly the same. Horribly so.
The host licks his fingers clean, which is a kind of finality.
We say *washing one's hands of it. Ethiopia* derives
from Greek and means *of burned visage*,
what Homer called *the sunburnt races.*
Sometimes, each breath burned to take in.
Sometimes, the fires started on their own.
It was all so beautiful it burns to remember.
At least I imagine the host that way. He is waving
goodbye to Pantelleria, perhaps forever,
though we cannot be sure. The helicopters circled.
The bombs hardly touched the earth before they burst
into white smoke. The host is waving goodbye
through the airplane's window, which must mean
another one is in formation, dangerously close,
as if there were another kind of nearness.

II

AERIAL

Heavy with answers, planes banked
toward the hillside, alive, on fire,
while my sister—all wedding gown
and shock—hovered over our pool,

in my friend's arms, on that threshold
between his drunkenness and the anger
of my mother, while the free world held its breath.
He didn't let go, though the ushers did

toss the groom and both fathers,
while the canyon offered its sparks.
For the most part, California was like that:
admixture of fear and celebration,

like root canals, or my father thrown
into our pool of meager wealth—
he of the bad back. Ash everywhere
but imperceptible. The grapefruit tree,

pruned violently, displayed its wounds
with an almost Eastern European sense
of inevitability, while bearded men I knew
before their beards danced with anyone

but their wives. The fires isolated,
my family threw everything into the day—
months of training, a fantastic processional
of rental chairs and dance floor, surrogate

flames of the chafing dish afloat
on sterno—our backyard some low deck
of the nearly tragic cruise ship, its fate
avoided at the final minute, anyway,

as the seaman waves, witness to the tip
of something on the horizon, bleak
and monogamous. Next day, my friend and I
raked our memories of domestic terror:

the saccharine Jordan almonds nestled
in pygmy hairnets, wads of chalk-white napkins
moldering like mice among the oleander,
and those uncountable aluminum cans,

spent shells on the last lawn I ever mowed
or mourned or swept clean of wedding flak.
In the distance, a plane spilled retardant,
returning empty, I supposed,

to its origin. It all seemed routine,
the violence that ignited each summer
in the San Gabriels, weddings attendant
to such eruptions of sage and scrub oak,

the bombardments, which reminds me:
first we peppered a lonely raft with cans
sticky and given to ants; then, being male
and stupid, we jumped in—I amid the bright

brand names, my friend under the diving board
he negotiated with my sister the night before.
While London could have burned for it all
front page and large enough the print ran

black in the eternal rain of my childhood
mostly spent in the dark shelter
of the Republican Party and wildfire ash,
in a suburb decadent enough to watch,

with no intent to punish, two teen boys
tread at opposite ends of a pool
and take turns pelting one another with cans
half-loaded with water, bombing

with the imprecision of bombers,
until the enemy surrenders, calls time-out
with blood on the temple, or at least
acknowledges by raising his hands

that he gives, really gives, then hoists
the white flag of my sister's dress
once, before placing her down,
into the arms of the late twentieth century.

FROM THE NEW REPUBLIC

The flamingoes in their carnival garb are plentiful
in plastic here. Trolling the meticulous Bermuda,
anachronistic, hieratical with their French-

maid formality, they keep one-legged vigil
at the fiercely contested and crepe-myrtled borders
of our collective happiness. Bewitched by the gazing

ball's stare among the pansies, we have come
to envy such stalwart defense of their own
frivolity, some home-improvement version

of the spiced apple garnish by the charred chicken
at the church luncheon, God bless. And though the sun,
for its part, might so lovingly tend to their backs,

compassion-driven, that composite seams
swell and blossom as for a surgeon curing
cancer, still those bleached, fist-sized heads

call from the mythic island of the herb garden,
amid the spidery hosta that rises like equity
each year, Miracle-Grown, ascends like saints

from the ash of martyrdom, to behold the world
they desired, verdant, bereft of pain, where hope
is a strictly outside cat, and love—love is money.

THE LAST CRUSADE

I was It, the unnamed, the great criminal
echoing a dead Venetian's name off stones
my friends' variously sized heads made

at water's rim. During the second golden age
of suburbia, I was blind but could speak
one word, *Marco*, to which the indigenous

quid-pro-quoed their *Polo*s before vanishing
beneath my dog paddle in the deep end.
Saracens, they gathered at the floodlight's eye,

or circumnavigated gunite, revealing
like vowels their inevitable emptiness,
voices mere mirage—islands I imagined

baptized in chlorine at the edge of the new world.
And since that world was cruel, I burned secretly
in the space between the game and my crusade:

to catch them slipping out, establishing outposts
at the far corners of the known, they
who simulated with mere hands a body

flailing. Ask any kid or medieval Venetian:
to cheat was nothing if not blind justice,
payment for our being born into savagery

masked only by the smell of gardenias
or the intricate shattered sea of a mosaic.
Meanwhile, I, the ascetic, the other, traveled

interminable routes strung in the silk
of my own wake, chased the disembodied
as they silenced, returned to the water itself

in that citadel of gated homes and oleander,
like saints who whirl in their church lazuli
eyes closed, perspectiveless, and hammered thin.

THE GROTESQUE

I am ten in my Sidewinder colors
at the Cineplex after soccer, gnawing
Milk Duds and grape licorice,
when Luke confronts Vader
in a swamp of Oedipal fantasy,
cow-eyed mask revealing the face
we all wore—an American sameness
that begets then kills itself in the hellhole
of Dagobah. This, before Freud, before
I caught myself in the polished marble
of churches I have been in (or made of) Italy,
before the grottoes, too, in Nero's villa
full of spindly arabesques, beasts
only Africa's rapture could contain.

What was later found there, in the spleen
of Rome, diggers labeled *grotto-esque*,
and again I glimpse the birth of a word
I thought I knew, rising from halls stripped
clean of sunlight, fountains run dry, all the way
to this campy patricide, this young Skywalker.
Is it any different? Surely in the Death Star
of his own self-regard, Nero must have loved
some version of himself resembling Luke:
boyish, touched by the force of gods,
or just the force that money makes, simmering
in its ledger.

I sucked at soccer, instead played
Luke to all the asshole Han Solos on my team,
who could head and deke, curve a corner
in the near side. In the team photo, I kneel
like a supplicant, squinting in the radiance
of early fall, California. Next to me, my friend Vince
(from *vincere*: to win), adept even at rest,
pitches shoulders back like a knack, a language
mastered long before we conquered all 320 steps
in St. Peter's dome, a decade after that snapshot
but millennia after Fabullus rigged for Nero
a revolving fresco, so the world literally turned
around the black emperor, perfume and rose petals
pumped into the least of his orgies.
                                        Not an orgy
but a bashing of the rival squad sent us
to a pizza joint, then to my third time
facing Vader and the vector of his weapon.
Is it wrong to say I envied him—Vince
and his right foot, rich parents, cool name?
The rich, too, have their suffering.
He's no Nero, anyway. Besides, it wasn't money
or power, the gall to watch his city burn,
so it goes, but the blessing Nero offered
his court architect, the shit-eating grin
when he said, with zero irony, *Build me*
something beautiful, beautiful as the Death Star
spinning its slow, clean banality, beautiful
as my friend, hands sticky with orange slices,
bending that corner right into the intricate net
that brought us, young men, to beauty buried
in Rome—breathtaking, I swear, those roses
falling in such numbers they could kill.

SOFT COSTS

Not the steel of real green, sweaty presidents
mutton-chopped and fretful, no fistful of ogling
pyramids or nickel buckshot the jackpot vomits.
Not the excruciating weight of the penny
lost below that '03 Yaris in the split-level,
its corrugated edges turning the cathedral green
of Danish copper. Not even the mother of all
those popsicle kids crowding the checkout line,
who waits for the register to end its refrains
before she plunges into her ludicrous purse,
slaps a checkbook open, and composes her elegy
to speed. (Behind the window of her license,
even the photo laments its holograph profile
of the state of despair they are all trapped in.)
Not any of that. Instead, think a pat of butter
slinking off a turkey thigh, the down of a cat
that naps your comforter to death. Think of comfort,
reliable excess, pleasure in that numbers game,
where the tidy ledger swells to blue and everywhere
leaks its secrets like the Camembert in its balsa
coffin, stinking of success, which is the smell
of putrescence. For now, some digits in the Beatnik
rant of your mortgage papers grow tired and old,
wear their trousers rolled, order the fish at four,
grow soft as lint in your pocket, which once
belonged to your shirt and, further back,
a farmer in West Texas, who at this moment
dreams of you amid his plush green field.

LABOR DAYS

I woke to a blizzard and franchise, burned
quickly the money earned in a strip mall
dress outlet, lugging vacuum into the Versailles

of a communal changing room. From my own face,
one hundred versions regressed in the netherworld
where underwear and slip seem not so much

confession as compression, those years I worked,
a layered look, simply keeping me warm.
Life's like that, stuttered the register.

It was California after all, where snow fell
only after baseball on TV—the Dodgers game
I watched, stunned by my first taste

of store-bought vacation. How eerily
the hours crept, imperceptible as the glacial
style that governs necklines, drawing deeper

into autumn's cleavage, the high arc
of the three-two ball lost in a spotlight
blur. Speaking of, years have passed

since I wrapped that vacuum's noose
around its neck and stowed it for the last time
in the history of Western civilization.

But for me, life really takes off in Rome,
in the Forum, when I watch a woman
stoop to the marble's face and read herself

into history, into that mirrored hallway
I see again as the door dinged
and women entered, purses slung over

their shoulders like recent kills. How many
tunnels back exist, as if we chose
from catalogs the clothes of our becoming?

I must have seemed strange, or worse, watching
her skirt-folds drape over marble, revealing more
than some unlikely blend, which is how life is,

and why, near the Vestal Virgins in the Forum—
millennia after the stones were laid, past trees
shorn of their spring collections, sinking

monuments, and history with its slick capacity
for erasure—I saw a dress shop, in California,
and the first full whiteout of my life.

III

WATERWALKERS

Erecting catwalks and scaffold over
the piazza at high tide, city workers glide
in orange-red smocks at the gates
to San Marco, transforming everybody

into waterwalkers: the tony waiter
wading the lagoon his patio resembles,
or the Japanese couple in a menagerie
of pigeons, even the masses in the atrium

under the shattered sky of a million tiles
in a Byzantine mosaic. In perspective's zero,
before creating depth, we were all split
in two. Jesus in the Jordan's vortex,

for example, all bone and angle:
there must be another side to this
rendering, to the curious gold pounded
into sweat at his nape, the water

swallowing him whole, until the other
self, incarnate, disappears. So it is
at the edge of the Western world,
this disappearing city, which renders water

that much larger that much longer, one more
fragment freighted out on the back of the sea.

Here, anyone can be beatified, anyone
with extra socks can cross the cramped sea

of tourism and mourning, float above
the sunken piazza, San Marco's warped floors,
and wonder at their bodies made numinous,
no matter how mortal they tried to stay.

THE BARISTA OF SANT'EUSTACHIO

Once, when he was young, he smiled.
A flat hand smacked him hard across the mouth.

He deals in darkness now, renders it less
solvent, poised for sugar, which he and no one

else incorporates. It is the only place in Rome
where this occurs, where this *can* occur—

the devoutness, I mean, with which he hates us,
froths our milk, his face in polished chrome

and pressure gauges. People come, for him,
in just two shades: dishonest and dark.

We are both—and foreign and Vandals—
or gods at least, who hoist the sun up clothesline,

carve out the hours of another ochre afternoon,
as the Pantheon cools, slicks from touch.

Surely he believes this shop a heaven for us all—
his condescension just some form of worship

mirrored by our impatience. We will wait
no longer for our kingdom. And he knows.

BELLAGIO

In another life, my bed is stripped of night.
Forgotten on the busy tile, bath towels reappear
the next day and the next, prim as morning papers.
But in this life, rain and petrol mix
off the ferry's stern, and a few men stare
at what I guess to be their pasts or a flurry
of gulls. It's that immense, that common.

The future, robed in morning chill, waits
at Bellagio, where tourists pick at the bones
of excess, and these men, I know, find lovers
on vacation, in rooms meticulous, feverishly clean.
But I have come in this life to sudden luxury:
a villa with a studio inside its turret, wine
nightly swaddled in linen, chilled like specimens,

and talk by a Swiss neuroscientist
on the syntax of dreams. And in that life
inside a scientist's dream of the perfect dream,
I descend marble stairs to the scent of basil,
lamplight blurred in fog, in his rigorous
ideal and demure left hand, which I studied
through his talk and momentarily loved.

Left, *sinistra*—a word with a dark sense
of humor, since he sat and listened to me,
kept motioning to, *Yes, bring more wine*
and *Please, go on, I'm enjoying this immensely.*

That night, immense and sexualized, I felt
ensconced among the garish flowers
in the baroque of his desire. I wasn't unique.

He claimed dreaming sex with hundreds of men.
Scrutinized like a leg of lamb, I couldn't hope
to brush myself from memory's gesso. Magnums
of Chianti. Those crumb-raking waiters. I sensed
that future undress me, the way the Queen of Night,
a viciously black tulip, if chilled, opens on command.
And after the ferry back, the boats poised

in surf like toys, I dreamed a man thrashed and gasped
in fishless waters. Beautiful in their lack, too humble
for more than luck, fishermen sat on a pier,
diagramming air around the flail. I could not tell
which one of us—the scientist or I—suffered
those men and stony silence. Only the gulls kept at it
all night, in their gibberish, at the borders of sleep.

WINK

In line for Nero's Golden House, my father
(white Reeboks and khakis, Nikon swaying
on its nylon strap) turns to catch the pomp
and whir of sirens, watches servicemen
like moths that mob the limo's flashbulb
nimbus. And when Silvio Berlusconi appears
booth-tanned and swaddled in his suit's
evasive discourse, when the magnate-cum-
prime minister (lecherous louse of a lost
empire buttressed by money and the butts
of his party girls) winks at my father
(In-N-Out t-shirt, knee-high whites)
my father winks back. This, when fate offers
small convergence, a *brush*, we say,
with the possible, stardom as a kind
of friction, a current powering our sad lives
in this sweltering afternoon in Rome
or anywhere. Because in that afternoon,
we are special, if only because this someone
supremely absurd but refracted through
the vast labyrinth of TV, a face as memorable
as cholera, ubiquitous and crooked like the many
towers of Italy, this someone deems us
worthy of attention, in all our garishness,
which is a kind of love, generous though
fleeting, that we could never give to him.

HOLE IN THE HEART

I have walked miles of decommissioned rails
in the hills above Spoleto, through galleries
perfected in the forges of archetype,
where bats fired like synapses. In any tunnel
or horror flick, this fulcrum, this choice:
to cover my eyes and march, or open wide
and return—to California, say, my sister
with her new twins two months premature.
In a photo, my father holds an infant in his hands,
and his hands are what I remember: inaccurate,
clumsy, too big to deliver anyone into this new
history of images. I have entered Italy through history,
from the otherworldly fluorescence of a bus terminal,
up escalators, through walls of a medieval fortress
like the one the mind makes of itself under siege.
When I emerged in the arterial confusion
of the city, I understood the Renaissance
in all its pomp and ephemera, each chubby cherub
suddenly airy, dumb from light. My wife and I,
childless, childishly watch TV each night,
talk to death our dedication to the image—
animal fetuses in vitro: the silky skin
of a wolf pup, hairless, eyes sealed over,
or rigorous organs beyond that briefest of feline
membranes. Surely we were meant to be gods
gazing through these windows at a heart
thrashing about like a bat in a tunnel in the hills
just north of Spoleto, where, in boar season,

hunters fire into the heart of autumn. Even in Italy,
I watched too much TV, conversing not with people
but with language itself. For hours the bright birds
of women pranced about some host—articulate,
bespectacled—who barked detergent. They are fine,
my sister's twins: Sam with tubes laid lovingly
in his ears. Lexi, a procedure to close a hole
in her heart. Imagine the lack of allegory there,
or in the way those dancers on Italian TV go under
for love of their bodies. Imagine sunlight
carving itself into Spoleto late, as I entered
over viaducts, not unlike a surgeon somewhere
in California, tunneling a blocked artery,
up a uterine canal, camera threaded in, back
to the beginning. Outside the tight gauze of the OR,
a few women in white gather. Cigarettes extinguished,
they also enter through a small hole in the heart.

THE CHURCHES OF ITALY

They are, like amusement parks, best
when almost empty. Like Great Danes
in dorm rooms, more impressive
for what surrounds, licking themselves
in the middle of it all: that broken piazza
and bad museum, bright shops
of potsherds and prosciutto. They are,
like horses in the heyday of Detroit,
beautiful in their uselessness. More
beautiful, in fact. Like damaged clocks,
they possess and are possessed by history,
stone still in all our million photos.
As if they never breathed. Uncanny,
aloof, they are aces at the sprawl,
laid out and loving it. We cannot help
but humor them, oil the great wheels,
crank them up so the engines sputter,
so everybody's hands wave in the air.

THE NEW WORLD

It must have seemed insignificant
at first, tiny imperfection in the glass
bowl of sky. Insignificant,

until the onlookers—not even flecks
in the bomber sites—realized what grew
fat on falling, expanded like the redwoods

I knew in the first years of knowing, ring
by ring. Insignificant, too, the shopkeepers
in hats, the lone woman picking capers

on the hill shot through with bunkers,
the whole of Pantelleria—clutch
of rock between Italy and the rest

of the free world—all witnesses
to the harsh conclusion of gravity,
bombs growing ring by ring, falling

like the memory of Sequoia I keep.
My father and I arrive at the cross-section
of a tree in California, to which he lifts me

and points. *Here, Rome burned, and here—*
his finger a ripple in the concentric archives
of terror—*is when they found the New World.*

Though by then, thousands of miles, days,
regimes away, only the plane's hum,
postpartum, in the horrifying science

of sunlight. The bombs, for their part,
surely meant the end of everything:
the corner stand selling cinnamon ice cream,

the corner itself, the man standing there
a moment ago, who will be found throughout
the twentieth century, whom I conjure

the only way I know—through my father—
and there before me in the rubble
of his future self, who has never seen

this island forged from my obsessions,
in the smoke that floated at the port
of Pantelleria, 1943, my father—a child,

but in this twin narrative, a man—
bends down, lifts me, places now
my finger on his chest ravaged by cinder,

a thing cut from a living thing, on display,
splayed out, touched by thousands of pilgrims
each year, and I look at him when I ask:

Is this what we looked like when we were found?

IV

OSSI DI MORTO

Hungarian-born Laszlo Toth took a hammer to the Pietà in St. Peter's Basilica, disfiguring the face of the Madonna and shattering the left arm. The assailant spent two years in an insane asylum, and the reconstructed Pietà is now shielded behind protective glass.

—New York Times

Consider the irony: *bones of the dead*
as confection, cookies piled behind panes
like those that separate the *Pietà*
in St. Peter's from the rest of the dying.
Because mostly in Rome, it is 1972,
as the hammer of a crazed geologist fell
on Mary, as he shouted, *I am Jesus Christ*—
believable in a country of children
craving bone-sweetness as prize for sitting
still as marble in the army of Sunday chairs.

When Laszlo Toth struck the Michelangelo,
shards scattered the floor, while gawkers,
the penitent, and even meek atheists in attendance
swabbed to catch a sliver quick under the skin.
They believed, for a moment, the flaw—their hands
snatching some flake of resurrection, mouths
in search of sugar they swore they tasted.
Some, like great palmers of the salad days,
brought back the forbidden rocks. Geologists
could understand the pressure, enormous
weight of splinters propped on mantels

in otherwise legal homes. Others never.
(Mary's nose, they say, recarved from a chunk
in her back.) I like to think I would be different,
could never even pocket a piece. Once tempted,
don't those witnesses still dream of the radiant
spark, like crushing peppermint in the dark?
On the other hand, to eye the sweets
in café glass, the drums of children's fingers,
some hardened part of me wants denial, burial,
each name returned. But how anonymous
that grate of teeth on bone and aching
flare of indulgence igniting everything
my mother swore would be the death of me.

LIMONCELLO

Brought to table shocked from frozen
slumber, ice-gauzed and ready to spill its skin
in the shape of private fog, it taught me
how wasting tastes—pungent, yellow fist
of a witch. In bottles whose necks are scarce
as Christmas in the Balkans, whose color reeks
like sadness dressed to resemble someone
almost famous, a lesser Marcello Mastroianni
or lovely monk grinding charity's gears,
who offered the lemon higher purpose, escape
from some sad buffet trout. Because my feet
weigh nothing after the climb to this osteria,
this bottle sweating its nimbus on mahogany.
More than the tibia-thin glass it frightens,
this detritus of citrus, sugar boiled down
to salve, pulls my mind into my mouth
like an itinerant dental hygienist
or my best blunders in the company of women
who summon limoncello from some Sorrento,
somewhere even maps might fear to rat on,
where the lemons, like cysts, slumber in neon
I could call death were I not afraid of dying
without first, then many times after, sucking
the life out, on this terrace, overlooking heaven.

BLOOD ORANGE

I palm and circumnavigate the sphere,
its helixed rind unbroken by the tilt
of knife I learned one night at table, mere
pivot of a Roman girl's wrist or lilt
in her voice nudging open the skin,
so it seemed, over the white mirror
of a plate. Her patience was its own
gesture, as was my watching her.

She could not have known, years before,
I treated clementines with the savage heart
of the heartless, the Vandal, more
intent to taste the ending than to start
with praise. But which is passion: to care less
for yourself or the time it takes to undress?

DISPENSATION

I followed you (not even sanctum
kept me) through catacombs
at San Sebastiano, the bleached femurs

shelved in mortar. Steeped
in our mandatory awe for death,
I fumbled with the buttons

of your blouse. You carried on parsing
Latin flourishes on marble, fingers
grazing the nude stone worn

by pilgrims numberless and sweaty.
Centuries later, we lie, lamplit,
shutterless, in a Roman hotel,

and I want you to know I read
often of God, skullfish in saints' books
and reliquaries, pore over ancient cities

exploding with promise of siege.
Those believers, little faith-labyrinths,
cannot be wrong. Yet how can I stop

thinking of the harsh trellis outside—
Moscato cloistering a fig, bees electrifying
the air, those bodies tethered to sweetness?

TRUFFLE

That piazza jammed with jowls of wild boar,
grappa-bottle boutiques, stacked baskets
of black truffle, and you in a dress, in my lore,
sifting through those stones. Ask if I could feel

a thing in the near-nil heft of the brown bag,
truffle inside. Ask what I remember at our sill
spiked to ward off pigeons—an autumn rifle
shaking you from me, while below the town,

headlights edged the cliff roads where hunters,
tourists, imagined some version of us. Not one
of them, of course, could sense this disinterred
knot, this moment ten years past. Now, two bowls

of pasta, cold-pressed oil, and this earthy cyst
all soft garlic and nostalgia. Can you feel
the absence in your hand, the weight of our amnesia?
Torn from rest, rooted by hounds, a truffle's right

for desecration. See how it grows ever more
precious, as if tucked under a bed like rations in war?
Now take the mandolin. Shave the tuber thin, pare
to skin, to revelation, which originally meant *disrobe*.

LITTLE SHOE

If you find yourself lost in the terrible
Mediterraneanness of exile, just sit
under the awning of an outdoor café,
somewhere not quite Naples but adequately

midday, with a Jack Russell terrier
named Damocles, and order the tart.
Admire the rain's signature on pavement
pocked with insignificant histories,

like the one outside Pienza after we stopped,
though broke, at the B&B to check the rooms.
You wore that street-market green blouse
bought from a man with his van door open,

and all those blouses (hundreds maybe),
and his kid, or whoever's kid that was,
above it all like a little despot with the tire iron.
And we of very little money, starved,

ate cheap pasta, believed in the zucchini,
like nothing we could ever find, nothing
we were used to, which left those little smudges
we took turns sopping up with bread

(*doing the little shoe*, they say).
I hope the wine is cheap and good

in the terrible Mediterraneanness of exile,
ruby in its fat-bottomed dark green bottles,

the same ones my mother used
for lemon juice. And the waiter
should say you are beautiful, though you
will not know. (You'll be staring conveniently

at sunflowers.) *Beautiful*, he should say,
in his starched, cultural distance, wanting
only to cover someone of his own
in a green blouse, and here you stumble in.

But he won't utter any of this
or the equivalent in Italian, and instead
just offer us the look that says, *Take care.*
And I have taken care that you should not

be exiled, though you must help me
with my fear of the terrible Mediterranean,
work off the idea of such terribleness.
You will have to be committed,

regular as sprinklers, or the smudge pots
in the lemon groves where I grew up,
sit me down with a glass of wine, nothing
too fancy, and say, simply, *Let's watch bad TV.*

And since I hate cop shows, the idea
of losing you should fade right into history,
like the Middle Ages and their fear of the fork,
which was—I swear I read—invented just for pasta.

SANTA MARIA IN TRASTEVERE

He tries to conjure Mary in the glittering
mosaic, her face a hundred tiles, stars
in the firmament of the apse. A halo, maybe.
He thinks of a simple courtyard barred
with iron. All the fastidious looking after
a church like that must see. Even the scent
he almost musters: toasted almond, cedar.

When he tells his wife, continents away, he's going
to Santa Maria in Trastevere for the first time,
she tells him he's been there, with her, twice.
He doesn't know what awaits him in the church
he's already seen, in treacherous Trastevere,
a name which simply means *Across the Tiber*,
a ten-minute walk from his rented room,
down streets he knows, toward the bright waters
of lapis lazuli he hopes will surround him,
in the church he has imagined, across the river.

NATIVE

Go back far enough, and nothing is native.
The bright globes of deep-fried risotto, say,
cupped in our hands on the ferry from Messina,
called *arancini*, little oranges, like those in the old
snake of Moorish caravans freighted with cinnamon
and clove: non-native as my unrolled *r*
in the word *arancini*, as you, on that ferry,
inside a train on that ferry, to be exact: all foreign.
Lover of origins, I imagine some merchant unpacking
crates off Bari or Brindisi, those outrageous yellows
and greens and, yes, the orange, spectacular enough
to claim its own color, its denial of rhyme, of corruption,
in English. Somewhere, that slice of navel
or tangerine, its pith and innards dexterously removed,
its juice a stain in the deepest creases of the palm
of the first Italian discovering orange, saying,
buona, buona, though that, too, is a rough rendition
of whatever he said in the long trajectory,
almost imperceptible, of nativeness. *Buon viaggio*,
they say, meaning good riddance, make way,
so long, all the way back to the late '70s,
California all citrus and condominiums
and what we called then *money trees*, silvery leaves
lacquered in mist. I could eat five, even six, oranges
straight from the branch without staining my shirt,
walk home on a stone wall slowly growing back
into the landscape, into my idea of landscape
more Italianate each day.

Today, for instance,
I find my old house in the eye of a satellite,
feeling the Braille of that suburban prose,
the subdivision and refrain of *money, money, money.*
I have never been farther away—that town a relic
now, rediscovered centuries later by the son
of a Venetian merchant struggling
to reconcile the endless Elm Streets,
Foothill Boulevards. He imagines a boy balanced
on a rock wall between two worlds: some pastoral
edition of his childhood called *Ubi sunt*, and the other,
America, named accidentally for an Italian,
a mistake now native to the land. *Native*,
akin to *nascere*, to be born, to rise
from that cramped sleeper, in that train,
in the belly of a ferry crossing to Messina,
to an upper deck, to behold Sicily
in its ascension from the horizon's amnesia,
the fruits of our travel southward fully in view,
and a man in white, who seemed to bloom
from the fluorescence above his metal cart,
who sounded perfectly native, of that place,
yet not exotic, not idealized, his apron stained
in saffroned sweat, his voice coarsest in its *r*,
which he rolled with such efficiency, calling,
Arancini, arancini, to no one, we thought, but us.

v

SURVIVAL ITALIAN

Carve away the bitter ends of verbs
like rinds from cheese. The word too hard to speak—
discard without a thought, like that robin
darting the maw of your mother's black
Caprice, the squirrel beneath your right wheel's love

of circular plot. Now penetrate the surface
comprehension—some lovers at the lido
and a blanketful of grammar. And why imply
your doubt with the subjunctive, when you can lie
on the coffin-narrow bunk in that rented flat

where the cat spritzed all your button-downs?
Why not become doubt itself, some faceless
version of you, floundering in the predicate?
Button up. For you can bear the lopping off
of proper conjugations, or watch declensions come

for visits, full of reticence and pocket change,
what little they can spare. The fishmonger might
despise your staring at the hollow eyes
of his branzino, at the unvoiced fricative
of the eel on ice. But luckily you know

the word for eel—*anguilla*—its dark melt
off the tongue, awful nearness to *anguish*.
Do you speak English? If so, it is autumn,
and a breeze flutters the leaves of your favorite
utterable lovelies, ripples the surface

of some *aperitivo*. How beautiful, how sinful
this country of your ignorance when toured
on Tuesday, say, devoted to the god of war,
when butchers sheath their knives, and televisions
spill the golden hair of afternoon

reports in waves you cannot grasp, but love
to be awash in, like a surfer in black who crests
a swell and feels the water an extension
of his body, then his mouth, hungering for more,
even when it doesn't know it's full.

BEFORE THE BOMBING

Before the bombing, there were photographs
of bombing, holes blown through
the immaculate white frames in textbooks,
where words gathered in the inevitable

euphemisms and epitaphs, which are the same.
Yet, to behold the planes in cursive encore
must have meant the end to rationing,
tautologies of newsreels, bland beans,

blackouts. Understand, the shattered
tenements, the dirty infant wail
of the many: these are a kind of good—
both portentous and capitalized—to sell

to the consumers of oblivion. No need
to test for dates, who bombed whom.
Because when we emerged, at recess, the sun
seemed utterly textless. Only prom slogans—

Remember Yesterday, The Time of Our Lives—
persisted, as if the past were just some neutral
state, a Switzerland of the mind.
Before the bombing, there were sentences

explaining crater, moonscape, a blank
where a church once stood, the pretty planter
in its place. That's how I later sensed
the past lingering in cobble and vetch—

Bologna's hillsides punctuated still
by unexploded mortars, flak and shrapnel—
and why some erasures mean the future,
while most just mean what came before.

PANTELLERIA

Its name fallen from Arabic and any love
of mutability—*Daughter of the wind*

relieved from the faces of postcards
in their wire bins in the bar at the end

of the broken promenade, even in script
angular and floating on the unreal sea

of that reconnaissance photo we saw
in the bookstore and were stunned by,

imagining the bombs in '43, plumes
like empty captions in cartoons, like the Trojan

farewell to Dido in her anguish, a goodbye
that sounded eerily like not sounding, not

saying, like the wind that stirs tonight
the chalk-white roads, a kind of bucolic—

not nomadic, Nubian or Eritrean, not
Abyssinian, but ghostly, elevated, of the epic.

Though at night, Tunisia turned its head to us
and winked, though what we ate, distinctly

Moorish, was unreachable—cinnamon and sage,
blood orange, the caper's pickled blossom—

still the sea never warmed those shins of lichened
shallows—black-blue, wine-dark waters cold

as late afternoons we consoled the abandoned
terrace, dreamed out past fantastic monoliths—

one resembling the elephant, might of Carthage,
its stone trunk arching over the pleasure boats, still

others guarded by water and the strict sentinel
of the tongue. We watched the sea hurry

these names on volcanic backs, our feet caught
in the Mirror of Venus—this, the name given

a lake of clay the turgid tourists
cloak themselves in, a lake that kept

birthing itself, white and white and white,
from whose shores we looked down

to the Bay of Five Teeth: pumice cones
of lava black as tar or a mother's midnight

voice calling to her daughter in the rip tide,
carried farther, beyond the cuttlefish

patrolling foam, the eel's soft suture
in water's skin. From far enough away,

even Dido looked content, inviting flames
to shake out sparks above her city,

as the tourists descend the mountain,
their children palled in the privilege

of this island, their small cars, humped
in baggage, lumbering down.

ELEGY

Is it remorse or remorse for feeling none,
empathy or its lack, compelling me again
to the port of Pantelleria, where we lost
ourselves in the sunburst of squash blossoms,
pistachios, the couscous in split Marsala casks?
None of this in '43, when our island, known
for capers, witnessed Operation Husky
and the new world of saturation bombing.
True, the olive trees genuflected sharply,
but only because of wind, which would not relent.
And the sheep's-ear leaves of sage we harvested?
They held but small vigil, sautéed in oil.
Yet on this island of regrettables, reduced
to rubble, relegated to those heavy winds,
elegies run wild by the roadside, low
to the ground, like capers, good for nothing
but the brine, and you pick them for free.

THE GRIEF INDUSTRY

To my nephew rummaging a sparrow
from the leaf mold in the neighbor's yard,
who loved it and the days he devoted
to its name, repeating to anyone

who listened—*sparrow sounds like arrow*
sounds like barrow—no wheelbarrow
could contain even the meager dead
of this yard, which is why I told him

of some heaven, holding the lie
up to the sun hanging over the trees
I lie by now, hanging much as ash
from the last cigarette all smokers know,

the eternal recurrent, the everlasting
last. Right now, my thoughts go out
to a thousand suns, as if sparrows
that will, no doubt, return. Why not,

as my nephew did, celebrate the end?
These days are so frightfully common,
so fastidious, I could not teach a clock to count,
so watch my neighbor tend to mounds

of leaves, nests in his fastidious lawn,
watch him pile each lot in a wheelbarrow,

plod to the curb. *Wheelbarrow*, I almost hear,
sounds like weeds buried, sounds like

we bury. My nephew, lover of construction,
boy who spent the afternoon consumed
by toy trains, establishing his depots,
delivering some economy of impatience

to the one village in our living room
that never finally incorporates:
he couldn't know, in Tarquinia,
the necropolis, too, began with travel:

the dead transfigured, made guests, invited
back to the cities of the living. And they came
in droves, almost manufactured, until
the living forgot which city was which.

So it is with rain: the more there is,
the less we notice. Once I watched men fire
blanks into the arms of live oaks in Texas,
scattering grackles. The day one fell

at my feet, I knew I was in love, at least
in its provinces—some backwater town
where death still sounded like breath,
and everyone lived on it. That didn't last.

Only a matter of time before the thriving
industry of grief closed its mines, its lobbyists
returned to plush settees in quiet stone
rooms, in Ohio somewhere. No one asked,

for example, what to do with the dead,
now that they were unnecessary, flat out

hated, had packed their bags and returned
to the Homeric epics, set up shop

on some island quarreled over by scholars,
where churlish gulls heckle in their vague,
unpleasant way. Used to be the dead
were nothing if not persistent.

Now, I imagine them lounging in the cool
of their shades, all grays and dark blues—
cement stained by gutter water, motor oil
on asphalt, the primered Olds that cruises by,

punches its Blaupunkt through the mist.
What's one more sparrow to the forest
of suicides or burning citadel, to Achilles
taking a drag off a last cigarette? Not even

a drag, this one small ending, and silent, too.
Like the underside of a threat or the over-gray
street after my neighbor beats back the fescue.
Yet, still I hear my nephew's Dada elegy—

sparrow sounds like arrow sounds like barrow.
Weeks later, the flies having issued final rites,
I continued—*sparrow sounds like harrow, sounds like
sorrow.* My nephew? He carried on with his trains.

ANTHEM

The last stand of Japanese maple
sheds its garments on the nature path.
In the distance, two retrievers race
between a fence's pickets. Their loose pelts
glide as they themselves glide, as leaves
scurry by the lakeside, headlong
into a certain future. Last night,
preparing hens, you lifted skin,
rubbed curry, olive oil.
The blind eye of the television
undressed the room as you undressed
the hens. Turbaned men and boys
with rifles, all in a veneer
of sweat and linen, sat in a circle,
eating. For the first time,
you used your hands. October,
and the neighbor hangs a skeleton
next to his American flag.
Shelter must have waited for the dogs.
When I stopped one, it was nameless,
as is the smell in the kitchen this morning.
Nameless, too, that faint sift of turmeric
into night clothes, haunting them
the way churches haunt their cemeteries.

EXILE

The bread of angels is everywhere the same.
The bread of Verona and Ravenna tastes of salt.

The distances, in other words, are immense. Jets
are necessary. Whole days in them. So much so,

if an osprey's cry punctures the air above my house
in epic simile, I cannot stop the inevitable

canonization. Which reminds me: a nuisance of cars
stopped last month for a dog. I alone returned,

got out, attempted the get. The dog had none of it.
Hubris, I mean. The kind exile demands. The rain

steady, a woman in boots and sadness got back
in her car. Or that was me and my feminine side.

What we go through just to feel sorry. Because
when I return home, evenings, I scan the street

for my dead cat who is not dead, and I'm surprised
every time. I want to be, at least. *The bread of angels*

is the same as saying *happiness is monochrome*,
eggshell white, which is not white, not calming, not pure

or innocent, but fragile, given to spidering, liver-spotted
and gumming up the perfect omelet morning.

I just want to remember this sun peaking over clouds
as I descend into Italy again. At least keep the name

of the attendant, who slipped me a second bottle,
alive. She made tolerable, somehow, the pathetic

brioche in its foreign cellophane, which is all
I can hope for in economy class, as if exile

could be managed by social institutions, as if
a jet, able to split open the sky and stop clocks,

were just another form of broken currency,
when I only want the clock to keep on going.

Other Books in the Crab Orchard Series in Poetry

Muse
Susan Aizenberg

Lizzie Borden in Love:
Poems in Women's Voices
Julianna Baggott

This Country of Mothers
Julianna Baggott

The Black Ocean
Brian Barker

The Sphere of Birds
Ciaran Berry

White Summer
Joelle Biele

Rookery
Traci Brimhall

In Search of the Great
Dead
Richard Cecil

Twenty First Century
Blues
Richard Cecil

Circle
Victoria Chang

Consolation Miracle
Chad Davidson

The Last Predicta
Chad Davidson

Furious Lullaby
Oliver de la Paz

Names above Houses
Oliver de la Paz

The Star-Spangled Banner
Denise Duhamel

Smith Blue
Camille T. Dungy

Seam
Tarfia Faizullah

Beautiful Trouble
Amy Fleury

Sympathetic Magic
Amy Fleury

Soluble Fish
Mary Jo Firth Gillett

Pelican Tracks
Elton Glaser

Winter Amnesties
Elton Glaser

Strange Land
Todd Hearon

Always Danger
David Hernandez

Heavenly Bodies
Cynthia Huntington

Red Clay Suite
Honorée Fanonne Jeffers

Fabulae
Joy Katz

Cinema Muto
Jesse Lee Kercheval

Train to Agra
Vandana Khanna

If No Moon
Moira Linehan

For Dust Thou Art
Timothy Liu

Strange Valentine
A. Loudermilk

Dark Alphabet
Jennifer Maier

Lacemakers
Claire McQuerry

Tongue Lyre
Tyler Mills

Oblivio Gate
Sean Nevin

Holding Everything Down
William Notter

American Flamingo
Greg Pape

Crossroads and Unholy
Water
Marilene Phipps

Birthmark
Jon Pineda

Threshold
Jennifer Richter

On the Cusp of a
Dangerous Year
Lee Ann Roripaugh

Year of the Snake
Lee Ann Roripaugh

Misery Prefigured
J. Allyn Rosser

In the Absence of Clocks
Jacob Shores-Arguello

Glaciology
Jeffrey Skinner

Roam
Susan B. A. Somers-
Willett

The Laughter of Adam
and Eve
Jason Sommer

Huang Po and the
Dimensions of Love
Wally Swist

Persephone in America
Alison Townsend

Becoming Ebony
Patricia Jabbeh Wesley

Abide
Jake Adam York

A Murmuration of
Starlings
Jake Adam York

Persons Unknown
Jake Adam York